T0198723

Taking a Journey into the

Emotions

of

Common Folk

B.G. Webb

authorHOUSE®

AuthorHouse™
1663 Liberty Drive
Bloomington, IN 47403
www.authorhouse.com
Phone: 1 (800) 839-8640

Published by AuthorHouse 04/24/2018

ISBN: 978-1-5462-3338-1 (sc)
ISBN: 978-1-5462-3336-7(hc)
ISBN: 978-1-5462-3337-4 (e)

Library of Congress Control Number: 2018903456

Print information available on the last page.

This book is printed on acid-free paper.

Dedication to Dolly Parton who sings about
the Common Folk of which she is.

Contents

Faith Station

Introduction

All aboard! The Golden Limited Memory Express leaves Penn Station in New York at 8:00 A.M. and takes the brave readers on a cross country journey to Los Angeles.

The train will climb high mountains, go through dark tunnels, cross wide rivers and lakes and cover miles of open land.

Beware! While the readers will experience wonderful feelings at some stations that will fill them with joy, laughter and awe, there will be other stations that will cause them to cry, sob and perhaps shriek in horror.

At the end of the journey the conductor on board the Express will help the readers understand what to make of all the emotions that were seen and felt at one station after another.

If you are one of those who shy away from emotions— especially painful ones — when don't get on board or if you are on board, get off now.

This Express train is only for the brave of heart.
ALL ABOARD

An Ode To Dolly Parton

Oh, Dolly you own
    my heart — my soul.
Yes, I'm in love with you
    Dolly Parton.

Ah, that Dolly sound
    is so heavenly.
The rhythm and the beat
    send me in any direction
you want me to go.

Yes, all your songs
    are great.
Why? Because they are about
    emotions we all feel.

Here are some of my favorites:
    "Coat of Many Colors"
    "Yellow Roses"
    "Wait 'Til I Get You Home"
    "Looking' Like That"
    "Take Me Back To The Country"

Your songs are about
    what all common folk experience —
love, disappointment, loneliness
    and broken hearts.
Oh Dolly, your sound
    makes us feel up or down
depending on the lyrics.
    Yes, I love when you belt it out —
loud and clear.

There are times when the
 lyrics are so sad that
I want to hug you and comfort
 you dear Dolly.

Yes, your country music
 give comfort and joy.
Your songs and voice reflect what
 all working people have
experienced and endured.

Dolly, may God give you
 a long good life
so you can continue to sing
 songs of the common folk.

WRONG STATION

The Man Who Sat in the Wrong Pew

Mr. Wood was his name
    and he got into trouble
because of all things,
    he sat in the wrong pew.

He had come from a
    farm family
that had settled in
    a town outside Moline.

He and his siblings
    were all successful.
He went into law
    while the others farmed.

His sisters all married
    well — business men,
teachers, lawyers and
    even doctors.

Mr. Wood became a
    leader in his town
and the owner of many
    apartments.

After he and his siblings
    lost their spouses,
he invited them to share his
    large home.

They all agreed
      and loved being
together again as
      they had on the farm.

They put on parties
      for the renters,
fireworks for the 4th of July,
      and pumpkins and cider
for Halloween.

The kids in the neighborhood
      loved Mr. Wood.
He would wave at them
      as he drove his '39 Buick.

Then it happened,
      the event at stirred up
discussion and gossip.
      Mr. Wood sat in the wrong pew.

One Sunday he decided
      to go to church.
It had been some time since
      he had been there.

He drove to the church
      and took a seat in a pew
—up close so he could
      hear the sermon.

He joined in as the
    congregation sang
"Jesus Loves Me" and
    "Onward Christian soldiers."

Several days later,
    he received a letter
reprimanding him for
    sitting in the wrong pew.

Well, you can imagine his
    surprise and shock.
He and his siblings had supported
    the church for years.

They often didn't attend
    services because of their
advancing years and
    difficulty in hearing and seeing.

He tried speaking to the minister
    but didn't get much sympathy.
All the neighbors thought it was terrible
    and sided with Mr. Wood.

He finally resigned from the church.
    He wrote that even Jesus Christ
himself would never go there if one
    had to sit in the right pew.

UNLUCKY
STATION

Uncle Junior

My father's parents married in 1912, when they were teenagers. The next tear my father arrived, and two years later a daughter was born.

My grandparents didn't talk about the early years of their marriage. In 1922, after years of allegations by my grandfather that my grandmother was stepping out on him, they were divorced.

Grandma had her share of boyfriends too. She told me many years later that they had been too young to get married.

Grandma, with the children, moved in with her parents. Grandpa went to Texas, where he married a woman who was part America Indian. They had two sons. The older one was named for his father, but we all called him Junior. His brother was named Joseph Benjamin, but to everyone he was Bennie.

Grandpa's second wife died of tuberculosis when the sons were toddlers. The boys were placed in an orphanage.

Later Grandpa returned to St. Louis and my dad was able to reunite his parents. They remarries and Grandpa's sons went to live with them.

In the summer of 1941, the younger boy drowned while on a summer outing.

After Pearl Harbor, Junior wanted to enlist in the military. Grandpa and Grandma resisted signing the necessary papers because they were still grieving for Bennie. They eventually relented and Junior joined the U.S. Navy in early 1942. I can vaguely remember when he came home on leave several months later. He looked so handsome in his uniform and photographs were taken.

Before he returned to base, he requested a rosary. We were not Catholic, but a neighbor gave him one. He kept it with him the rest of his life.

Junior was assigned to the South Pacific. In December 1944, my parents received a Christmas card from him. He could not say where he was stationed. He could only say he loved his work and that he was very busy. He also mentioned that he missed the winter snow of St. Louis.

His rank was Aviation Radioman Second Class.

On December 20, 1944. His plane left the Mariana Islands to participate in a search reconnaissance mission. During a bombing run on the Caroline Islands, the plan was hit by enemy anti-aircraft fire and plunged into the ocean. His body was never recovered. My grandparents were notified that he had been declared missing in action. On January 5, 1946, he was declared dead as of December 21, 1945. He was only 20 when he died.

I wrote to the Military Personnel Records Center in St. Louis. I was informed that he had won the American Area Campaign Medal, the Asiatic Pacific Campaign Medal and the World War II Victory Medal.

Uncle Junior's name appears on one of the tablets in the Court of Honor across Chestnut Street from the Soldiers' Memorial in downtown St. Louis.

As I trace the name August H. Middleton, Jr. with my finger, I think back to the time he was home on leave. I feel very close to him and I sense that he knows that I am thinking about him.

I am the only living relative that remembers him.

I often wonder what he life would have been like if he had lived.

I recently played our video tape of the movie *South Pacific*. In the opening sequence, some radiomen are in the plane over the Pacific Islands. I cannot keep from thinking that these men might have been Uncle Junior.

BLACK STATION

The Girl Who Dreamed She Was Accused of not being Proud to be Black and Beautiful

Oh no! I'm back in my
    American Problems class.
And I can't believe it —
    there is LaTasha who was
so mean to me.

And next to her is Larry —
    the president of the
Back Students for Awareness
    and Action.

Ooh I've got to wake up —
    this is a nightmare.

Oh my God, Latasha is looking
    at black guys who have been dating
white girls. She speaks:

"You Black men have been brainwashed
    by the white dominated society
to believe that Afrian women are not
    beautiful. You want white women —
especially those that have Nordic charactertiscs —
    I'm talking about the blonde, blue-eyed
creatures that dominate the world of advertising.
    Well, I'm here to tell you that
I'm an African woman and I'm Black and Beautiful."

Oh No! Now she is glaring at me.
    She shouts: "And, you. Anna, think
you're better than me because you have
    lovely straight hair and cream
colored skin — you are accepted by
    many white students because
you look like one of them — White and
    Beautiful.

Well, I going to tell you how you got
    that way —- Your grandma was raped by
a white slave owner — yes that's that happened.
    And the result is that you are not
proud to be Black and Beautiful."

    ANNA WAKES UP IN A PANIC AND

THINKS: "Boy that LaTasha could scare the living shit out of you!"

BLIND STATION

Surrounded by Fog in
a Sighted World

I feel as if I am walking around - literally - in a fog. I hear voices, but I don't know where they are coming from. I see shadowy figures, but I don't know who they are.

Diabetes is an insidious affliction. It is robbing me of my eyesight. I have a wrinkled retina in one eye and cataracts on both eyes, but the doctors refuse to remove cataracts because of the risks due to diabetes. Nothing can be done about the retina.

I have sought second and third opinions. Stronger lenses in my glasses would not help because of the cataracts. Doctors tell me the only thing I can do is keep my blood sugar under tight control with lots of exercise and a strict diet. No wonder I sometimes get depressed.

Diabetics must test their blood often. I have trouble seeing the drop of blood and the small area where it goes on the test strip.

Being diabetic means a rigid lifestyle. There is little room for spontaneity, especially for one who hates schedules.

There are stages of grief: disbelief, denial, anger, self-pity, coming to terms, acceptance and learning to cope. I am going through these stages because I have a loss - my sight. It's like losing an old friend.

Right now I am in the anger stage. I ask, "Why me? I didn't ask for this."

As if don't have enough problems, I must deal with the reactions of others. I've noticed that if one is sick, people tend to run in the other direction, for fear of being asked to do something. When one loses his/ her sight, people run away faster and farther. They probably fear the unknown and don't know what they can do for me. I guess they are reminded of their own mortality.

The loss of sight brings about other losses. I can no longer drive a car, use a computer, do a jigsaw puzzle, go to a store by myself, read a newspaper, read music, hold a job, prepare a meal or do needlework or crafts. I have totally lost my independence.

I am like a six-year-old. I can dress, feed and bathe myself; but I can't prepare the food, see the colors of clothes or apply my makeup.

When I go out, I have to be accompanied by a sighted person, who 99.99% of the time is my husband, Bud. I have a white cane to help me with steps and curbs.

I cannot see facial features clearly. I need to be six inches away from a person to see him or her. I rely on voice recognition. God only knows how many acquaintances think I have snubbed them.

I try not to focus on what I cannot do, but what I can do. I am trying to adjust and become more independent within my foggy world.

I have magnifiers in every room and in the car. My easy chair is as close to the TV as possible. I eat from a dark-colored plate because most of what I eat is light in color.

I have a calculator and telephone with large keys. I memorize the number of steps from one place to another, as well as the location of keys on the TV remote, microwave and telephone. I put my many pills on a white paper towel so I can see them.

I sought help from the St. Louis Society for the Blind. They have support groups where I have met others in my same situation. I learned the fundamentals of braille.

The Wolfner Library in Jefferson City, a subsidiary of the Library of Congress, provides books on tape, postage free. These tapes are a real Godsend. They help pass many lonely hours. I have "read" about 120 books in the last year and a half.

I must say the world could make itself more "blind - friendly." At the Art Museum, for example, the guards are constantly reminding me to "step behind the line." I simply moved closer to read the tiny plaque beside the painting.

There should be a law that all lettering - print and on TV - should be in black on a white background. And it should be in LARGE LETTERS! Fancy script should be outlawed.

I am slowly learning to live in my foggy world. I rely more on hearing, touch, taste and smell. I am reviving interests I had before the fog sidetracked me, such as writing.

I have not lost the ability to think and to string two or more sentences together. I keep reminding myself that the great poet John Milton was able to compose Paradise Lost when he was blind by dictating it to his daughters. Bud is my secretary/transcriber, another of his many duties as my caregiver.

I feel I am making progress. It is a learning experience. As Eleanor Roosevelt said, "We learn from living and experiencing both the good and the bad."

MURDER STATION

Why did it Happen to Frankie?

Frankie was such a beauty
    with her radiant smile
and gorgeous figure
    which she displayed with pose.

Oh God, why Frankie?

She had the most lovely sounding voice
    that gave one reassurance.
And, her laughter would light up a room
    with warmth and joy.

Oh Heavenly Father, why Frankie?

She had a caring heart
    which she showed in her
devotion to those in need of
    emotional support.

Oh Almighty One, why Frankie?

She was helping friends
    when it happened.
Off for a short outing to
    celebrate their friendship.

Oh Jesus, why Frankie?

Then he attacked them,
   tied them up,
   beat them before he
raped them.

Oh Christ, why Frankie?

When her body was found in the snow,
   she was bound with ropes.
Her beautiful face was gone,
   replaced with blood and bone fragments

Oh Father in Heaven, why Frankie?

Why do bad things happen
   to good people like Frankie?
Why wasn't she protected by
   a caring Father in Heaven?

Why? Why? Why?

Do you exist dear Lord?
   When people pray are you there?
Did we create you to give us comfort
   in this brutal world?

Oh great Mighty One, why Frankie?
   Why dear, caring Frankie?

LAUGH STATION

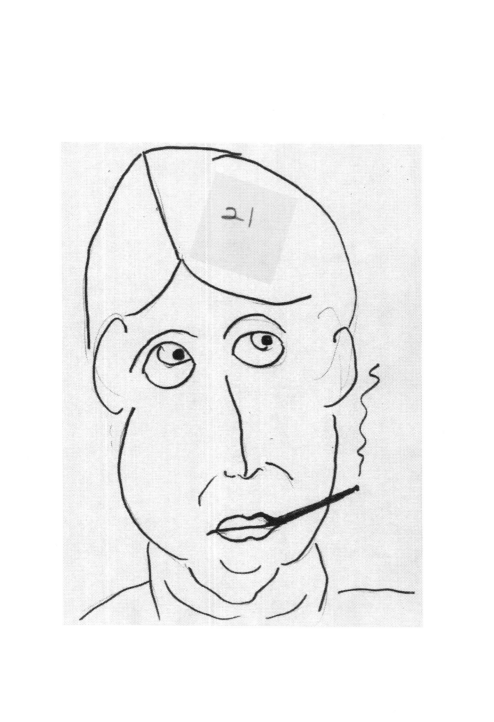

Okee does a Gig at the 007 Club in Chicago

Pussy Galore:
"I want to introduce
Okee Penokee who will
give you a lot of laughs.
He recently appeared
at the Prick and Ball Club in L.A.
So, give him a big hand!

Ya hoo! Ya hoo! Ya hoo!
(plants in the audience)

"Thank you! Thank you!
And thank you Pussy for
for that great intro.
Don't you love Pussy?
What a gorgeous gal! What a
bosom! What a rear end!
Laughter and Ya hoo! Ya hoo!
Back stage I gave her a
big hug and a kiss.
I love to kiss Pussy.
Laughter and Ya hoo! Ya hoo!
Boy, this is the first time
I've played in Chicago.
I bought a Grab magazine when
I got off the jet. Lot's
going on here. Wow!
Ya hoo! Ya hoo! ya hoo!

Hope to give you lots of
belly-laughs tonight.
Laughter brings sunshine into your life.
Right?
That's right!
(a plant in audience)
Even doctors say that laughter
helps you stay healthy.
Of course, I would add fun sex too.
Right?
Giggling and (a plant That's right Okee!")
I'm starting off with a song
and a dance. Can't sing.
Pretend I'm George Burns.
(Okee does a soft shoe and sings "There is no
business like show business."]

Applause and Laughter
(from a plant in the audience)
How is your love life Okee?
Not so good. I dated a gal by the name of Anna.
She was a ballerina from Russia.
Liked to make love naked while high on her toes.
Had a great time with her.
My love-handle can reach very high.
Laughter Ya hoo! Ya Hoo!
But then she wanted to screw while on
the balancing beam.

Well, I fell and broke my leg.
Had to say goodbye to
Anna.
Laughter and Giggling
Then I went with Judy who was a
construction worker.
She was sexy in her orange outfit.
Had a bubble ass and
gorgeous red hair. She was hot!
Laughter Ya hoo!
Yes I really had a passion for her
But, she liked rough sex.
After awhile I felt like a road
under construction.
So, had to give her up.
Laughter Giggling
Foks, you may not believe this
but I was hired at a sex
clinic to help people who had
sexual problems.
We met in a circle
and shared problems.
You know, people can be so
cruel.
One guy said that his date told him,
"I've seen joints bigger than that."
Laughter

Then one gal said that a guy looked
a her bosom and said, "Boy,
your tits are so small. They look like
lemons"
Laughter Giggling
Anther dude said that he was too big.
Yes folks he showed us.
His dick was like a child's ball bat
and his balls were like tangerines.
Laughter Laughter
We all agreed that maybe a specially
built robot would be the
answer to his problem.
Well, later we found that he
had done that. Yes, he named her
Rita and she can take his
package. And, ladies and gents
Rita can really suck.
Giggling Laughter Ya hoo!
Oh, something wonderful happened
for me.
The Trojan Company asked me to
come up with a slogan
for a proposed National Condom Week.
I want your input. Here are some that
I've come up with:
Don't be silly, protect your willy.
laughter

You can't go wrong if you shield your dong.
laughter
If you think she's spunky, cover your monkey.
Laughter Giggling Ya hoo!
Well, it's time for the intermission.
Have some drinks now.
Or do some stand-up dancing.
Hey, there is also the back
room where you can have some fun.
(Okee sings "Wait Till I Get You Home ")
and does some more soft shoe as
he leaves the stage.
Applause Applause Applause

UNFAIR STATION

The Lady Lost Everything
but her Courage

She had just finished a short prison
    term when she came to live
with us in our small upstairs apartment.
    She only had her purse and a
suitcase with her make-up kit and a change
    of clothing.

My mother welcomed her
    without hesitation
despite other relatives shying
    alway from Ethel.

But my mother
    loved her sister
and seemed to understand
    how events are
beyond our control.

You see, dear reader,
    Ethel had married
a man who robbed and
    stoled.
When he police
    arrested him,
they also arrested
    Ethel.

They accused her of
    knowing and indeed
helping him pull off a
    lot of break ins and
robberies.
    So, she was sentenced
to a prison for a year.

    The tragedy was made
worse by what
    happened to their
two children —
    Jimmy and Sharon.

Both were sent to an
    orphanage.
Sharon was nine and
    Jimmy was seven.

After a year in prison,
    Ethel was released.
That's when she came to live
    with us in our
small apartment.

She lived in our attic.
We partitioned
    part of it off
to make a small
    room for her.

But, the attic was cold
     in the winter
and hot in the summer.
     But, Ethel said it
was o.k. — that she opened
     the window or put
on more comforters.

She got a job
     as a waitress.
She had a radiant
     smile and was
still very attractive.

She spent a lot of
     time on her make up.
You see, she had been
     burned on her
face when a gas stove
     had exploded.

She would set up a
     mirror and her
make-up kit in our stairway
     hall and spend an
hour putting on her make-up.
Once I opened the door
     and the mirror fell down.

This startled her,
    but she called me over
gave me a hug and said,
    "That's O.K. honey,
I'll survive."

As a child, I often wondered
    what she thought about at nights.
Here she had lost everything —
    husband, two children and
had a prison record. Plus, many of
    her brothers and sisters
had turned against her.

But, she hadn't lost courage.
    By the way, she always put on
a brave front. She was a great actress.
    She would smile and laugh and
say that "things will work out."

Then, one day she was
    informed that her daughter
Sharon had been adopted by a
    wealthy farm family.

Jimmy wasn't as
    fortunate.
Why? Because he was slow.
    So, people didn't want
to adopt him.

Despite this bad news,
    Ethel kept smiling and
pretending that she was going to be alright.
    She even dated an older guy
who had taken a shine to her.

After a year of living with us,
    she went back to DesMoines.
She later got work at the
    Veterans Hospital.

In 1947 she met an older
    but wonderful man
by the name of Chester.
    They were married
and hoped to regain custody
    of Jimmy. But days
before it was going o happen
    Jimmy died.
About a year later,
    Ethel was able to see Sharon.
They arranged secretly to meet at
    the Iowa State Fair.

It was a very emotional meeting.
    The two were silent for
a long time and then embraced
    and cried.

The first thing Sharon said,"Wish
        Jimmy were here too."
Ethel replied, "He is here if only
        in our memories -
in our hearts,"

I have a black and white photo of
        Sharon and Jimmy taken
before the tragic events that changed
        their lives forever.

There we see two smiling
        children under a shade tree.
They are smiling as if they have just
        enjoyed a laugh together.
They seem so happy and safe,
        unaware that events were
going to happen that would
        set them on a path not to
sunshine or darkness of the Black Moon.
        No, they were to be trapped
in semi-darkness — in moonlight.

COVER UP
STATION

One Husband – Two Wives

My parents never should have married. They did not get along, and I wonder if they ever did love each other. Each was looking for a way out of an unhappy home situation.

Years ago there was a radio show about a couple names Bickerson. That show was about my parents. They bickered about everything.

They argued about whether my brother should be part of a drum-and-bugle corps, about her cooking, about who was the better driver, how they should spend money – the list goes on and on.

Their biggest fights were about religion. They had met and were marries in the Southern Baptist church.

Dad had developed diabetes in his 20's. He later had heart problems because of it. I now know that he didn't feel well much of the time, because I am encountering some of the same difficulties.

Dad hoped for a divine healing and turned to the Assembly of God church. He went regularly and Mom wanted to go with him. Dad referred to their bitter fights over religion as the "War of the Roses" and claimed they made about as much sense.

My mother was the original "control freak." She felt as if was her duty to manage everybody's life. She considered herself an expert on everything.

Mom and Dad split up briefly – several times. One time he moved into a boarding house, and she cross-examined the landlady about his comings and goings. He was a lawyer, and she had his secretary stop by the house on the way home to report on all that had gone on in the office that day.

Finally, dad had enough. He moved out for good and filed for divorce. They had been married and fighting for 30 years. They had recently relocated to Chicago from Belleville, Illinois.

A month after the final decree, Dad married a woman he had met at his church. Mom was flabbergasted. She felt that no woman would ever want to marry him. All she saw in him were his faults.

Dad took his new wife to visit all the relatives. And everybody said they had not seen him so happy in years.

Life is hard to figure out. A year later, dad had a massive coronary and died. He knew that my mother, the controller, would try to get his body and bury it in their plot in a Belleville cemetery. But he had told the second wife that he wished to be cremated at once. They were all living in the Chicago area at that time.

Mom called me with the news and said there would be a funeral in Chicago. She wanted me to put an obituary in the Belleville newspaper. But she insisted that I list her as the widow. Wanting to avoid conflict with her, I consented. Looking back, I realize now that I should have refused her request and forced her to find someone else to lie for her.

Bud and I raced to Chicago only to learn that cremation had taken place.

I had never seen my mother so much at loose ends. She had lost control of Dad, and did not know what to do. Besides that, she kicked herself for not staying with him so that she would have inherited all his money.

What she did was call Belleville cemetery and have the marker put down with his name and the dates, her name and birth year and the words "Together Forever."

I'm sure the second wife never learned of this.

Mom dies four years ago and is buried to the empty spot where she wanted dad to be. There she is all alone, with no one to control.

If she is in heaven, I'm sure God is telling her, "now listen Missy, I'm in charge here."

GOSSIP STATION

The Unforgettable Aunt Rose

Visiting my Great Aunt Rose
    was always an eye-opener
To a boy of eight
    who really knew little about life.

She seemed so special.
    Why, you ask?
Well, she lived in a suite
    at the LeClaire Hotel.

Also, she had traveled
    throughout the world.
You see, she had married
    Larry who was with the
Boston symphony.

The company of musicians
    toured the world giving concerts.
So, Rose had been to London, Paris, Berlin
    and even Rio and Tokyo.

She kept up with world affairs.
    Since she was a strong Democrat,
she would not read <u>The Chicago Tribune</u>.
    Only <u>The New York Times</u> would do for her.

Her suite was filled with moments
    that she had gathered —
a statue of Buddha, an ebony African
    figure, a fan from Japan,
And large vases from China.

She had met some of the leaders
    of the world and had strong views about them.
"F.D.R. was the most charming man I ever met."
    "Hitler was nothing more than a Charlie
Chaplin doing a stand-up routine."
    "Mussolini was a fat, greasy pig."

One of the things she loved to do
    when I would visit was to get out
her large box of family photographs
    and tell all the skeleton stories.

I can hear her now:
    "Maude's husband was a bootlegger."
"Clarence got syphilis and had to be
    committed to an asylum."
"Alice was so dumb that she went off to
    Reno to join her no good husband
who was a professional gambler."

Rose was very much against
    a burial of a body.
So, when Larry died, she
    had him placed in a
niche at our local mausoleum.

Then, to my surprise, she
    said that she had seen Larry.
I listened as she described how
    the casket was rolled out
of the niche.

She described how the lid was lifted
        and then said, "Larry was just the same.
He looked so nice in his pin-stripped suit
        and his polkadot bow tie."

Aunt Rose was quite a
        colorful character.
She is now in a "drawer" next
        to Larry.

I've never had the urge
        to go and see her again.
I'm quite content to
        remember her exotic suite,
where she voiced her strong opinions,
        told all the family secrets,
and made me feel like a world
        traveler.

LESBIAN STATION

(Delores is the one on the left)
A salute to a brave lesbian!

A Salute to a Brave Lesbian

Delores was her name
        and she came into
this world and was confronted
        with challenges
not of her making.

She was born to an
        unwed mother
and then adopted by a
        couple who had lost
an infant son.

While her parents loved
        her, they also told
her over and over that they
        had wanted a son.

Delores was never told that
        she had been adopted.
But, it became clear to those
        around her that she had
been or that something was very
        wrong.

Why you ask?
        Well, for one thing she
was very tall and looked nothing
        like her parents.

By the age of 17,
    She was 6'3" tall
and was described as
    being "handsome."

As a child to please
    her parents she liked
to dress up like a boy
    and act like a son.

She went out for all
    sorts of sports - -
baseball, tennis, track and
    even basketball and
wrestling.

After she graduated from
    high school,
She joined the Waves much to
    the delight of her parents.

It was then that she
    learned the truth.
It came out during the
    enlistment process.

Was she upset?
    you bet she was.
But, she learned to
    cope and move on.
Besides, there was a war to win.

So, Delores was sent
    to the Pacific theatre
of the war and served
    with honor and courage.

She saw a lot of terrible
Things out there
As our troops skipped-hooped
From one island to another.

As a Wave she did what she could
    to help and comfort
our wounded soldiers and others.
    she was awarded medals
of honor to reward her for her efforts.

She never talked about it - -
    but once in a while tears would
fill up her eyes as a word or
    action would bring back
dark echoed and shadows of battles.

During the war she met and
    fell in love with
another gal who had experienced
    many of the things that
Delores had faced.

They found good jobs and set up
    housekeeping in San Francisco
and later took in Delores' mother
    after she lost her husband.

Delores never held grudges or
    spoke of what might have been.
No, she took each day as it came and
    was thankful she had found a
"wife" who truly loved her.

When she was told that she had cancer
    and did not have long to live,
she got busy and took her mother back to
    Iowa to be with kinfolk.

She was so efficient that she paid
    for the care and burial
for her mother so that other relatives
    would not have to worry about anything.

Delores spent the rest of her days
    enjoying the company of the love of her life.
And being thankful for being able to meet
    the challenges not of her making.

We didn't speak much about Delores
    after her death.
All through her growing up years she
    had seemed queer and odd to us.

Then, one day we saw an episode of
    that TV Series entitled,
Queer <u>As</u> <u>Folk</u> and we thought about
    Delores.

That series helped us understand her
    better and we suddenly began
to appreciate her more and even
    to salute her courage.

We Salute you Delores!

AWE STATION

The Stripper Named Trixie

There once was a
stripper named Trixie
who worked at the Club
Flamingo.
Drummer: Boom da Boom! Boom!
She shared her dressing room
with ten other strippers.
She loved the guys
in the band — often
shared "joints" with them
and if they were good
— very good, they were given a
good night with Trixie.
Drummer: Boom da Boom! Boom!
She was billed as
"the powder puff girl."
Why? Because she came on stage
only with long gloves and
a large powder puff.
Drummer: Boom da Boom! Boom!
The band played Strauss'
"Wine, Women and Song"
as she did her exotic and sexy
routine for the mostly
male audience.

Drummer: Boom da Boom! Boom!
She would swing her hips
to the left — then the right.
She would turn around and
wiggle her behind.
Drummer: Boom da Boom! Boom!
Then, she would coyly remove
her gloves with an impish grin.
Then as the guys cheered,
she dropped the large powder puff.
Drummer: Boom da Boom! Boom!
As the guys went wild,
she swung her hips to the right and left.
Then she slowly removed the powder puff
on her left breast —
then the one one the right — and then
with another impish grin
swing both at the audience.
Drummer: Boom da Boom! Boom!
Her finale was really something.
From a small basket
she picked up tiny powder puffs and
yelled, "Come up and give
Trixie a pat on her behind.

Drummer: Boom da Boom! Boom!
Well, the lucky guys
who had caught the puffs
were delighted to come up
on stage as Trixie turned
around and received
pats on her behind.
Drummer: Boom da Boom! Boom!
Then, Trixie said sweetly, "Oh thank you gentlemen.
Thank you gentlemen for that patting."
And, then she dropped the powder puff
that covered her love-tunnel
that had been pinned to her G-String.
As the guys went wild with
passion and cheered her performance,
the lights went off and Trixie
disappeared,
Drummer: Boob da Boom! Boom!
(back stage) Well, Mr Benson, (prop man, age 63) did I give them some
sunshine?
Miss Trixie, you sure did. Even I got a "heart" on.

The Latino who became the Star Stripper in all the "Hot" L.A. Clubs

Tony Costello was
    his name and
he danced and stripped
    at all the "hot"
clubs in Los Angeles.

Tony was the son of a
    drummer from Brazil
by the name of Francisco
    Costello.
So, he grew up hearing music.

His mother was a popular singer
    by the name of Delores Rio —
whose real name was Delores Smith
    from Cleveland, Ohio.

Francisco and Delores had met
    while performing in the
same night clubs in L.A. and
    fell passionately in love.

Well, their passion led to
    the birth of Anthony
who was called "Tony" by all.
    He inherited all their talents
— a sense of rhythm, love of music
and a voice of a Elvis Presley.

Besides that he inherited all the
    good looks of his father —
tan skin, black eyes and
    a wonderful smile.

Oh, I should add that he was
    6'2" tall and had a
"package" that other boys
    envived because it
was long, thick and had a head
    the size of a golf ball.

Yes, indeed, Tony had it all
    — looks, talent and well hung.
    When he was in P.E. playing
basketball, his manhood would
    often be seen seen dangling
    out of his jock strap
when he jumped up to make a basket.

When he turned 18, he decided
    to join his folks in Show Business.
He became a male stripper
    at the night clubs in L.A.

Why a stripper? Well he thought
    that would make him a star —
someone special. He tought, "With my
    looks and long cock,
and dancing ability, I would be a
    SENATION in capital letters."

As the band played "Runaway Train"
    he did his number.
He used two costumes — a cowboy outfit
    for the gals and a Batman outfit
for the guys who went to gay bars.

As he danced on stage as a cowboy,
    he took off the following
and threw them to the audience:

    leather gloves

    leather vest

    leather pants

He was left with his mask, cowboy hat
    and G-string.

As he arched his butt toward the
    gals, they would slip bills
in his G-string.

For the guys he did the same
    routine and only left his
cowl on and black G-string.

Well, Tony was a sensation.
    By the way, he wasn't gay,
but a job is a job.
    The slogan in the biz. is:
"Accept a gig anywhere as long
    as you're paid."

As he became known for being "Mr. Big",
     he sometimes found notes with
phone numbers and big bills and offers to
     pay him more if he showed up to
lay the signer.

Well, Tony's view was: "If the offer is good
     and the gal/guy is hot, why not.
It's show business — got to please my fans."

In his mind he was a STAR —
     SOMEONE SPECIAL
     A SENSATION.

PET STATION

The Dog who thought he was the Coach of the Saint Louis Cardinals

Dakota was his name
    and he thought he was
the coach of the St. Louis
    Cardinals.

How did he get that
    illusion you ask?
Well, he owed it all to
    his owner whose
name was Dorthea.

Yes, Dorthea first made
    Dakota into a fan
and then his ego took
    over after that and
he thought he was the
    coach of the team.

It didn't take Dorthea
    long to transform
Dakota into not only a fan
    but a coach as well.

You see, dear reader, he had
    all the fine qualities
that a Golden Retriver is
    known for:

intelligence,
confidence,
trustworthiness,
kindness,
and
friendliness.

And, besides that he was like
     Dorthea — had redish brown
hair — appeared as alert as a
     red cardinal in spring.

Yes, Dorthea would hold
     Dakota close to her
in front of the TV during
     game time and then
before each inning sing:

"Take me out to the ball game,
Take me out to the crowd,
buy me some peanuts and
     crackerjacks,
I don't care if I never
     get back."

During the song,
     Dakota would smile
and howl with his deep voice
     at the end of each
joyful stanza.

Then, he would be
    rewarded with crackerjacks
from a bag that Dorthea
    had been enjoying.

Of course, she bought a
    Cardinal cap and
an XXL Cardinal shirt
    for Dakota to wear
for each game and around
    the neighborhood.

When a Cardinal player
    hit a home run,
Dakota would smile and
    howl with delight.
Of course, Dorthea would
    give him a big hug and
lots of crackerjacks.

However, if a player
    would strike out,
or be sent to the dug out,
    Dakota would bark
and jumped up and down.

Yes, Dakota was well known
in his part of town
for being a Cardinal fan and
coach, with a keen instinct
for predicting the outcomes
of games and who was
going to the World Series.

When Dorthea took him
around the neighborhood
dressed in his Cardinal cap and
shirt, neighbors would
ask, "Well, tell us Dakota,
whose going to win
this Saturday?"

And Dakota would tell them.
If he barked a lot and wagged
his tail, it meant a Cardinal win.
If he lowered his head and put his
tail between his legs, then it meant
a defeat for the Cardinals.

You may not believe this,
but Dakota was right all of the time.
Yes, he was a brave and loyal Cardinal fan
who had the keen instinct for the game
that would rival King Solomon at bat.

LOVE STATION

Nothing Like being in Love with Love

I love being in love with love.
    Why? Because:
        the heart beats faster,
        the mind become dizzy,
        one becomes ticklish,
        and you find that you giggle at lot.

It comes in stages.
        First, one becomes attracted to another's lips, hair, ass, etc.
        Then, comes the first touch.
        It's like being hit by lightning.
        That leads to the first kiss — then touching nipples, face, penis,
        vulva, etc.
        Then comes the interlocking of the naked bodies— followed by the
        rush of ecstacy as both lovers reach climax.

Where does it take place?
        On a dance floor
            or in a shower
      or under soft blankets,
            or in the backseat of a car
      or anywhere — anytime.

What emotions result in this passion of ecstacy?
        Here is a list:
            feelings of oneness,
            complete physical pleasure,
            light headedness,
            promising anything,

spiritual bonding and
BEING IN HEAVEN.

Oh, there is nothing like finding another who is willing to love, love, love
—YOU AND ONLY YOU.

Yes, there is nothing like falling in love and sharing the physical and
emotional feelings of love.

Yes, indeed, there is nothing like romantic love that is also combined with
physical pleasure.

Oh, there is nothing like falling in love —with LOVE.

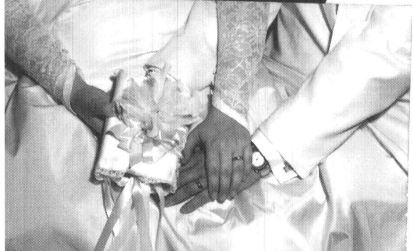

Two Boys in Love

We met at the U. of I.
and fell in love.
We were drawn together
by our mutual male needs.
We were very different,
in so many ways.
Jawaharial was from
an upper caste from India.
I, Buddy, was from the blue-collar
class of the U.S.A.
While he was a Hindu
and had grown up along the Ganges,
I was a Christian who had
grown up along the Mississippi.
Jawaharial was tall,
muscular and black.
I was small, white and
had blue eyes and
blonde hair.
While he was well educated and
had seen the world,
I was poorly educated and had only
been to DesMoines and Chicago.
Despite all these differences
we became lovers.
Why? To meet our male sexual
needs and to give each
emotional support.
He seemed drawn to me
because of my blonde hair,

blue eyes and boyish understanding
of life and the world.
As I would dress, he would
laugh and say, "Your pubic hair
is blonde too I see."
Sometimes, when I shaved, he would
appear behind me and say, "Stay still,
let me see your beautiful
blue eyes."
For a long time, I felt that
I was living with a Negro.
Over time, I realized that I
was living with a highly
cultured prince of India — a maharajah.
He loved to make me
laugh by tickling me.
He would smile and say,
"You Americans are like the
English — so serious —so up tight."
Our relationship changed
when I felt his naked body
up against me at night.
He held me in his strong
arms until I yielded to his
sexual needs.
He smiled as he
played with my penis
and ass, and put his soft
hands around my waist.
His black skin felt like

black velvet
and I relaxed and felt secure
in his embrace.
Then, he whispered in my ear,
"I'm going to give
you a gift from the sacred
waters of the Ganges".
Still holding me firmly,
he slid his head under the sheet
and placed his lips around my penis
and then gently began
sucking.
I felt such pleasure —
such a feeling of esctasy
that my mind became light
and dizzy.
When I came
as a result of his soft
black lips and tongue,
I felt a calmness, a feeling
total tranquility.
Then he turned me over and
came between my thighs.
As he did he gave out a sound of
pleasure.
We layed together for a long
time, knowing that two
boys had become lovers.
Then we got up playfully
and rushed to the showers where we

laughed and soaped each other.
Over the next two years
we repeated this act of love.
Where?
on the athletic field at midnight
along the beaches of nearby rivers and lakes
in one dorm room after another
in one of the upper floors of the stadium
in stalls in bathrooms at Lincoln Hall
in the university library surrounded by books.
Why? Well, our passion became overwhelming. And
the different locations made it seem exciting.
Jawaharial took it upon himself
to educate me about life.
He spoke of the rituals of his people —
of life along the Ganges.
He spoke about the teachings Hinduism —
of reincarnation and even the art
of lovemaking.
He showed me ancient carvings
of male and females figures in the
act of making love in various positions.
He said that I must experience love-making with a woman like he
had. Then, we will talk about it. He said sex with a man or woman is
wonderful. But, each has its own pleasures.

He said, "The act of love between human beings
is sacred. It is the species' way of meeting our sexual needs. Love in
any form is a positive
way in which humans give each other
support, pleasure, release. It is a gift that we give
each other"
Yes, the black boy from the land of
India had taken the white boy with the
blonde hair and blue eyes and had guided him
out of the darkness of the black moon
into the sunshine.

NEIGHBOR STATION

In Praise of Good Neighbors

Many believe that a person lives as long as he or she is remembered by others.

I hope it is true because I want to perpetuate the lives of many of my old neighbors in Moline.

Why? Because of their caring attitudes and good deeds. So, here goes. THANK YOU. THANK YOU SO MUCH —

To Irene Johnson for helping me with my Latin and taking me to see my first vaudeville show in Davenport.

Mrs. Applegate showed her love and understanding of children by popping popcorn for me and other kids and allowing us to sit on her front porch and have a party.

Arvid Israelson gave me my first paying job of cutting grass and showed me by his example that a warm outgoing person can have quite a positive impact.

Thanks to Dorothy Johnson for teaching me and others how to get on with your life after suffering a loss — in this case the loss of her husband at the Battle of the Bulge.

I am grateful to Mr. and Mrs Kloster for being the master and den mother of Cub Scout Den #12 and helping me and others earn merit badges and for letting us use their big yard to hold neighborhood circuses to raise money for the Red Cross.

Florence Smith showed me how a person can help someone who has lost a loved one by simply volunteering to do any household chore that might be of some help.

George Wood was a kind landlord who took an interest in his renters and planned neighborhood parties for them.

His brother Fred Wood taught me all about planting a Victory Garden and at the same time a reverence for the soil.

I appreciate Caroline Israelson for teaching me to go to the rescue of those in need as she did when she heard the screams of a neighbor who found herself trapped after a window had fallen on her hands.

Thanks to two very old ladies who everyone called "Grandma Benson" and "Aunt Rose" for showing how you accept adversity and the harshness of fate. They lived in an upstairs flat and supported themselves by Grandma making and selling throw rugs and Aunt Rose cleaning offices in downtown Moline. Despite their own hardships they were known for always giving a kind word and a helping hand to others in the neighborhood.

Last but not least, Herbert Webb, my father, who never charged his neighbors for starting their cars because as he put it — "it isn't a neighborly thing to do."

And my mother, Dorothy Webb, for having a warm smile and a sympathetic ear for every person in the neighborhood. THANK YOU. THANK YOU SO MUCH!

May you all live forever in the minds of all who read this. You practiced the Golden Rule in thought and deed and deserve to be remembered.

40

1808 1st Ave

1812
11ᵀᴴ Ave.

41

RESCUE STATION

Sisters of the Precious Blood

Sisters of the Precious Blood

Martha was only 18
when she heard the
voice of Jesus telling her
that he needed her.
    Jesus, we hear you,
She asked the Lord why
and what would she do.
He said that she would help
those who were in
physical and emotional pain.
    Jesus, we hear you.
So, Martha joined an Order — the
Sisters of the Prescious Blood.
During the ceremony where she became
a bride of Christ,
she heard the vows of the order:

    care for the sick

    defend the oppressed

    give comfort to the lost

    pray for all in need.

    Jesus, we hear your prayers and commandments.

As she did her work among the

German people,
she became aware of the attacks
    on Jews.

        Oh Christ, we will find a way to save Jews.

She and other members of the order
    were shocked by:
    the arrest of Jews

    the attacks on Temples

    the open killing of Jews

    the death camps.

        Oh Jesus, give us courage to find a way.
All the sisters prayed with their Rosaries
        day after day
for Jesus to give them a plan
    of action - a way to
    save as many Jews as they could
    and especially the
children and babies.
        Oh Jesus, give us a way to recue Jews.

Then, one day the answer came
    to sister Teresa.
She received it in a dream
    in which the sisters
    disguised themselves by becoming
    medical personnel.
        Oh Christ, thank you for showing us the way.

So that is what they did —
    medical uniforms of various types
were obtained.
    Some of the convent's autos
were changed to look like
    Red Cross vehicles.

        Oh Jesus, protect us as we try to save Jews.
When they would arrive at a
    site of an attack on Jews,
they would look for the children
    and babies.
They would gather them up in
    their arms and tell the
Nazis that they would take them
    into Custody.
        Oh Dear Lord, be our protector.
Those who were saved were
    taken to the convent
or a church to stay until they
    could be taken out of
the country by train.

        Oh Jesus, watch over us.
Most were taken to a railway
    station and given to people
who pretended to be their
    parents for a journey
out of the country.

Oh Christ, give us strength and courage.
As the children were handed over
   a sister would always kiss the
child on the forehead and cheeks and say,
   "Auf Wiedersehen mein liebes Kind."

Hallelujah! Hallelujah! Another saved.

Oh Jesus, we are doing the work you commanded us to do.

We, your brides will fullfill our vows that entitle us to be

SISTERS OF THE PRECIOUS BLOOD

WHY STATION

Why did it happen to Ken?

Ken seemed to have it all.
    He had a good paying job
at a local foundry
    with a pension plan.

His wife was a beautiful
    outgoing gal.
who had given him two
    children and plenty of support.

When it came to church,
    he was there every Sunday.
He believed that Jesus
    was the Son of God.

He read the Bible too
    and prayed to the Almighty
for the souls of others
    and for the recovery of the sick.

Then he was killed
    at work.
As he was returning to his work bench,
    a heavy piece of steel fell on his head.

All were stunned.
    They asked, "Why oh why did
this happen to Ken?"
    Oh Jesus, why him?"

His wake was so sad.
    There was Ken in his casket.
There was the grieving widow
    and her crying children.

All wondered why God Almighty
    had allowed this to happen.
Even the minister couldn't explain
    why bad things happen to good people.

Even today people remember Ken
    and ask the same questions.
Even today they realize what was
    taken away from him.

He never saw his children
    grow up.
He never enjoyed the company
    of his beloved wife.

Why dear Lord did you take him?
    Did you need him more
than his family and wife?
    Why oh Heavenly Father, oh why?

The Man that said, "We All Screw Up Sometimes!"

My Uncle Chester was
quite a guy.
Not only was he tall and
handsome, he was also
a very wise man.
He gained his wisdom
not from any fancy college,
but from the world of hard knocks.
He had three favorite expressions:
"Life is messy!"
"Shit happens!"
"We have all screw up!"
As a youngster,
I didn't buy into any of the above.
I felt that if person planned,
took care, followed the rules,
everything would turn out fine.
Well, as I lived in the
real world, I found out
that Uncle Chester
knew what he was
talking about.
I found out that
life is messy
because we have very
little control over
people and events.

He pointed out that he
didn't want to kill people but
he had to during World War I or
a German would kill him.
He also said that he believed the
first woman that he would have sex with
would be his bride-to- be and not a French
whore. But, when he was stationed
in France during the war, he needed sex
and he thought that he might be
killed at any time — so he thought "what
the Hell, I might as well get
some real loving before I die."
Chester also pointed out that if
other people don't change,
then you do. He declared, "Humans
are constantly in the state
of changing and becoming.
That's life!"
He freely admitted that he had made
a lot of bad decisions — had
screwed up. He even listed some:
too much drinking
too much drugs
too much unprotected sex.
He stopped doing these things because they
did not give him the happiness he
he was seeking.
He pointed out that we learn from
out screw ups.

He also said that everyone had screwed up
and if they said "no" it meant the following:
1.They were habitual liars.
2. They lived in a make believe world.
3. They were prisoners of social customs.
4. They feared the punishment of God.
5. They feared they would lose their jobs
or elections.
He had a passion for telling the truth
about members of the family.
He also liked to read obituaries and then
point out what they left out or
covered up.
Well, life has taught me that
Uncle Chester was right.
We all screw up. Life's messy
because we can't control
events and other people.
And, I found that, like my
uncle, I learned from my mistakes.
Yes, life is messy and I'm proud to
join Uncle Chester and admit
I have screwed up — big time. And
I have learned from my
screw-ups.

BULLY STATION

The Boy who had to Run and Hide

THE BOY WHO HAD TO RUN AND HIDE

There was a boy
    who feared the outside world.
Why? Because of bullying
    He seemed weak to others
because of the effects of having
    rheumatic fever and rickets.

"Girly, girly, you are so cute."

Because of his medical problems,
    he did not have the energy
level of other children.
    Others, especially other
boys and girls could not understand that.

    "You are a sissy - a girly boy."

They thought that he should be like
    his brother who was tall,
athletic and into all kinds of sports.
    Yes, even teachers said to him,
"Why can't you be like your brother."

    "Hey you sissy, I'm coming after you.
    You better run — and fast too."

He seemed queer and odd
    to many — the way he used his hands,
the way he walked and his interests
    in arty things.

"Hey girly boy, show us your pussie."

Many called him "Sally"
    and made fun of him.
Some girls refused to speak
    to him because he seemed
queer and odd.

"Sally, Sally, show us your panties."

Also, some of his odd ways were caused by his
    mother who kept telling him that
she had hoped to have a girl before
    he was born.

"Sally, Sally, skip like a girl."

In order to please her even as
    a child he would wear dresses
and play with dolls. Why?
    Because he wanted to please his
mother and be the child that she
    longed for.
Once he even prayed to Jesus to
    make him into a girl.
Yes, this boy was all screwed up
    by things that he did not understand.

"Hey girly boy, you can't play with us."

The bullying got worse when
    he started junior high school.
When he was in grade school,
    he got along with most of the
boys and girls.
    And the teachers would not
tolerate bullying.

"Sally, Sally, how about a kiss?"

In gym, it was especially hard
    for him to put up with the
teasing and name calling.
    He felt so alone and defenseless,
especially when the teacher did nothing
    to stop the bullying.
    "Hey Sally, you better make a run for it."
At home, things were bad.
    His dad started drinking heavily
and his Christian mother who had always told
    him not to use his fists,
became seriously ill with high pressure
    problems and depression.

"Sally, Sally, show us your tits."

He began to hate school —
    gym, lunch room time,
everything about it.

So, he started cutting gym
which was at the end of the
    school day.

    "Hey girly boy, we are going to beat your ass."

At the end of the term,
    he hid in the hot attic
where he could escape the
    mean world and the bullying.

He found it difficult to talk
    to his parents about
the problem because they had
    problems of their own.
In a way, he felt that he had to
    take care of his mother —
and protect her from his dad who
    often abused her.

    "What can I do? Who can I turn to?"

The thought about going back to
    school was horrible.
So, at the end of the summer,
    he decided to kill himself.

He got a rope and made
    a noose and then
he tossed the rope over a
    beam in the attic.

He stepped on a chair,
    put the noose around his neck
and stepped off the chair
    and within 5 minutes
he escaped the world of
    bullying.

Yes, he was free from a world
    that is brutal to
those who are odd, queer, strange
    and different.

He was only 14. Think of all
    things he missed.
Think of all the wonderful things
    this arty boy may
have contributed to this brutal
    world to make it more
wonderful and humane.

COURAGE STATION

Our Brave, Courageous Belinda

My wife Louise has a cousin
named Belinda
and she is battling the horrible
thing called MS.
She is a beautiful petite
lady with red hair,
blue eyes and a warm smile
that often is the start
of a laugh or giggle what
lights up a room.
When we speak of her,
we often say, "So
how's our brave and courageous
Belinda doing?"
We use the words "brave and
courageous" because
that's what it takes
to deal with MS.
There is no known cure
for it now.
As the victims' condition
gets worse and worse,
they have to rely upon the
kindness of people,
their own courage and faith
that God will help those
working to find a way to cure it — so others
will not suffer as they do.

Belinda was still in
the first grade when
the muscles in her arms, legs and
spine began to weaken
and shrink.
When her parents took her
to the doctor,
he diagnosed the condition
as MS.
She noticed a lack
of coordination,
clumsiness, inability
to work or climb
stairs and difficulty raising
her arms over
her head.
Unlike many who have MS,
she was able for a time
to lead a fairly normal life.
She even married and
had children of her own.
Then, in her forties,
things got worse.
She had to use a walker
and a motorized
scooter to get around.

When she would get into
her van, she would
approach it
backwards—
using her walker as support.
She approached steps
the same way — backwards.
With her van she was
able to attend
church, club meetings and go
to the store.
She even taught
a Sunday school class
for some time and she
was secretary for
family reunions.
She had to use a pencil
to type
and later for using her
computer,
but it worked.
She would hold the pencil
in her teeth and
then start typing away
letter by letter.

Yes, Belinda has had
to show a lot
"get up and go" and
inventive ways to do
the normal things that
other people
do everyday.
Belinda doesn't live in
the future.
No, she takes each day
as it comes and
thanks the Lord for helping her
come up with new ways
to fight the crippling effects
of MS.

GRIEF STATION

Danny is the one on the left

Danny, We Miss You So

It came every summer
and with it fear, panic and heartache.
We kids called it polio,
and were terrified of it.
Danny, we miss you so.
Part of the fear came
from not knowing what caused it.
I can hear the warning now:
"Buddy, don't go to the swimming pool."
"Stay clear of ground water and sewers."
"Be alert to those germ carrying
flies and mosquitoes."
Danny, we miss your impish ways.
We all knew the dreaded symptoms —
high fever, stiff neck, painful muscles.
We knew what they led to —
paralysis and then the "iron maiden."
Danny, we miss your giggling.
The "iron maiden" was what we called
the metal casket-like tube that
helped your lungs. None of us wanted to
be trapped in that container.
Danny, we miss our rough-housing.
Then in the summer of 1944
it happened — Danny got it.
He went fast —
he only lasted a day or two.
Danny, we miss your silly grin.
We were stunned.

"It couldn't be Danny," we all thought.
To us he was the picture of health —
robust, always running around.
He was energy personified.
Danny, we miss your playful ways.
The funeral was private.
Why? Because people thought that
he ws still a carrier and one of
us might get polio from him.
Danny you were our buddy, pal, friend.
All his Cub Scout buddies
were invited to attend a special
memorial service for him.
His parents were presented with a
picture of Christ knocking on the door.

      Danny, we will miss you at Boy Scout meetings.

It was a beautiful picture
but it wasn't Danny
with his smile and boundless energy
running around the play ground
at Willard Grade School.
Oh sweet Danny, we miss you so.
I remember sitting in the pew and thinking
"God, why did you let this happen
to Danny? He was my pal, my buddy,
why dear Lord did you take him?
Did you need someone to give you a
smile and a laugh?
Well, Danny can do that and a lot more.
I hope you like to play kick-ball,
because Danny sure does.
          Danny, my buddy, goodbye old chum!

Grief and Relief

You have just gone thru the ultimate tragedy.
You have seen the great love of your life to the end.

First you realized that something was very wrong,
Then came the endless medical parade,
The doctors, the hospital, the tests and more tests,
The treatments tried and the treatments abandoned,
The hopes raised and the hopes dashed,
Then the inevitable pronouncement,
"We can do no more."

All the weight of the family fell on you.
You managed all, his part and yours too.
You cared for him as you could, and
Then arranged for more care.
You supported him and he died.

The grief and relief both came.
The relief does not lesson the grief,
And the grief does not condemn the relief.
Let them both fill your very soul.
Only then can you heal,
Heal and rebuild.
There is life left for you.

Learning to Walk Alone

We got our signals crossed, Lorraine did not go with me.
I went alone to the Garden.
Yes it was better to go alone for the first time
But I was so alone!

Before, I would occasionally like to go somewhere alone.
A sense of freedom went with being by myself.
Then I was alone by choice;
Now I am just alone.

I watched the other walkers as I had never watched them before,
Family groups, young couples, pairs of women and old couples,
Oh the stab of jealousy when I see an old couple.
But no men without woman or child.

As I neared the Japanese Garden I saw another lone woman
She looked as miserable as I felt. Was she crying too?
Then as I neared the pool by the Climatron,
Another lone woman, and she smiled at me!

It was a cold wintry day; nothing would be in bloom.
The winter aconite? No, the Woodland Garden is blocked off
But wait, there they are, the spring Witch Hazel is in bloom!
Spring will come!

I will not try to avoid places we enjoyed together
No need to learn to be alone. I am alone.
Friends can often fill the empty feeling,
But I must learn to walk alone.

The lady who always wore black

Caroline was her
name and she
always wore back
where ever she went —
stores,
churches
weddings
visits
etc.
She was a teller
at the U.S. Bank
before and after
her marriage to
Patrick. She wore brightly
colored outfits
that were beautifully
coordinated
with shoes, purses, scarfs
and everything else.
She was a beauty
with her lush black hair,
blue eyes and gorgeous
figure that were
a match to her smile that
seemed to light up
every gathering that she
attended.

How did she come to wear
black you ask?
It was the war — it changed

everything.
You see Patrick was killed
during the Battle of the
Bulge and Caroline lost
what gave her that
radiant smile.
Caroline never got over it
— the telegram that he was
missing — and another
that he had been killed.
After that — the return of the
body — or what was left of it —
and the burial in the military
cemetery at the Rock Island
Arsenal.
She dressed in black
for the funeral —
black veil and gloves —
everything in black.
She literally became a
shadow in black.

She stood by the grave
as taps were played
and rifles fired.
When it started to
rain, she found herself enclosed
in black umbrellas
raised by kind souls who wished
to protect and hug her.
Afterward she found herself
locked in black —
locked in morning for Patrick.
Infact, she found
comfort in the darkness —
it enclosed her and in some

strange way brought
her comfort.
You see, dear reader, she and
Patrick were a perfect match.
When they said "I do" their
souls were forever unite.
The phrase "until death" didn't apply
to their special relationsiip —
they were eternally united.
At their wedding they truly
became one spiritually.

Some criticized her for
morning so long —
for not getting over it
— that wearing black
made others depressed.
Caroline turned a deaf ear
to those remarks and
continued to wear black
for the rest of her
life.
Why you ask?
It was the only way that
she could cope with the
terrible loss of the
love of her life.
Much later, when she was
dying at a nursing home,
she told her kinfolk, "Dress me
in my wedding dress when
I'm in the casket. I want to
to surprise Patrick
when I see him in Heaven."

FRIENDLY STATION

It's a Long Way to Quincy, Ill if you don't have the Cash

Tim and Meg
had lost their way
when they showed up at
our doorsteps.
They didn't have the
money to get
to Quincy to stay
with kinfolk.
Since we had known
them before the war,
mom and dad invited them
to stay the night.
They had their two
children with them —
DiJoe age 10 and
Jimmy age 7.
As mom set up cots
in our small apartment,
we listened as they
told their story.
Tim still couldn't find
a job as a mechanic.
He had gone from one dealer
to another — no luck.
Being in the army hadn't
helped him much.
He basically worked as
a kitchen helper at

the mess hall.
He met a lot of others
guys like himself
who hadn't been able
to get deferments.
I was shocked when he said
he had been stationed
close to an all
Negro division.
He laughed when he said that
the guys in his unit liked
to take turns shooting at the
"niggers" as they
went to the outhouse.
As dad and Tim drank
whiskey and beer chasers,
mom counted up the money
we had to help the family
pay for the train fare to Quincy.
The next day after lunch,
we drove them to the
R.R. station. Mom paid for
their tickets and then
we sat and chatted until the
train arrived.
When the train arrived,
we went with them to the
platform. We wished them good luck
and hoped that Tim could
find a job.

Before they boarded,
mom smiled, hugged Meg
and handed her a basket
of sandwiches and apples
for a snack on the long ride.
As the train pulled out,
we waved and wished them luck.
Then, we got back into the car
and headed back to our
apartment.
We were silent as we drove
back up the hill to our place.
In our minds we were all thinking,
"That could be us."

LOST STATION

The Boy who could Hardly Speak

The boy who was lost in silence and
hardly ever spoke was Johann.
He was found wandering in a German
death camp after the war.
Of course, the authorities
knew he was a Jew.
But, he seemed to be in a
state of shock.
He was lost in silence.
When they tried to find out
about where he had come from,
who his parents were,
he remained trapped in silence.
He had a number tattooed
on his arm but it did
very little in helping the
authorities find out
who he was.
The Germans had destroyed
the records of the Camp.
They assumed that his
parents had been
separated from him, gassed and
their bodies had
been cremated.
So, eventually the authorities
gave him the name of Johann
and found a Jewish family
in the U.S.A, who wanted
to adopt him.

I met Johann when he joined
my 6th grade class.
By that time he had a last name
too — Johann Shumann.
Before he arrived Miss Anderson
told us about Johann
and where he had been found
and that he spoke very
little English.
The next day in walks Johann.
He was dressed in blue overalls
and had a sweater on that featured
red and blue stars.
He was small, had large back
eyes and on his cherub-like
face an expression of bewilderment
and fear.
Johann's arrival in my class
brought the horrible realities
of the war home to me. Here was a
living example of what evil
things can happen to the
innocent.
Up to that time the war had meant
these things to me:
flattening out tin cans for the metal drive.
seeing news reels at the movies,
preparing Red Cross boxes for those
in the war zones,

hearing about my cousins who were
fighting overseas,
organizing Victory circuses to raise
money for the Red Cross,
Tending our our Victory Gardens,
and dealing with ration stamps for gas, etc.
Now, in comes Johann to my classroom.
His appearance made the war real
to me —the suffering and insanity
of it all.
When he started to speak in his broken
English, he made mistakes or
sounded funny.
Some would start giggling — even
laughing at him.
At that point, Miss Anderson would say,
"Now children, don't do that.
We must help Johann in every way.
Your laughing wouldn't help."
Well, guess what happened.
Johann blossomed with
all of the help we and his adopted
parents were giving him.
He still didn't smile much.
He never did remember his
parents or what his life was before
the camp.
All that was locked away
in darkness.

Perhaps it was just as well.
Perhaps, that was how
nature helped him cope and
survive. Who knows?
Yes, Johann became our
buddy, our pal and friend.
Then one day on the play ground
while we were playing
baseball, he was up at bat and
hit a homer.
It was then that he suddenly smiled
and laughed.
We all shouted, "Hurray for Johann!"
As he stood there with
a big smile on his face, I thought,
"Johann is part of us now —
and while he isn't home yet, —
        he is on his way."

The man who was only seen at night.

I was told
    that his name was Fred,
the son of the custodian
    at Willard Grade School.

Nobody ever saw him
    except at night
when he would leave his
    parent's home and walk
around the town.

No one ever talked
    about him.
His life's story was
    covered in darkness
and told in whispers.

I only found out more
    about him as a result
of running into him one night
    and then asking Caroline,
our next door neighbor
    about him.

It must have been
    9:00 P.M. when the "Night Man"
(that is what the kids called him)
    practically collided with me
along the tree lined street.

I remember hearing his
    steps in the Autumn leaves
and then seeing the silhouette
    of a tall figure coming
suddenly toward me.

He had a cap on
    and wore a black trench coat
and I called out "Hello!"
    He responded with silence —
he simply glided by me.

Later, I would be told by
    Caroline that he had been born
to the Smiths in the 1920's
    and was mentally retarded
and hence remained at home.

I often wondered
    what he did all day long
in his 2nd floor room in
    the frame house that
the Smith's owned on 12th Ave.

I never found out.

    The "Night Man" continued
to be seen by a few — walking
    in the darkness — forever
lost in his dream world.

    Perhaps, the only sounds he
ever heard were the rustling of
    Autumn leaves and the
hooting of owls.

FAITH STATION

Two Angels Among Us

There are times when
I believe that angels
of the Lord come down from above
and dwell among us.
One, of course, thinks of:
Jesus
Buddha
Gandhi
Mohammed
Mother Theresa
John XXIII.
We had out own angel
in Moline, Illinois.
His name was
Campbell Bailey.
We always called him
Rev. Bailey,
because he tended the
flock at the
First United Presbyterian Church.
He was married to
another angel of the Lord
by the name of Minnie
who helped him tend the sheep.
As a child,
often wondered
if God Almighty had sent
them together to help
the lost folk of our
town.

Rev. Bailey did all the usual
things expected
of a minister:
sermons
baptizing
marriages
raising funds
supervising the Sunday School
classes.
funeral services
But, Rev. Bailey and his wife
(or should I say angel) did more
than the above.
What? Well, they became
part of the common folk.
Yes, when they visited
your house
(and they did so often)
they pitched right in
and helped you with
your shores.
If you needed help
washing dishes,
Rev. Bailey would grab
a T- towel and help.
If you needed someone
to help hang out the
clothes to dry, Minnie
would help you.

If your furnace needed
more coal,
Rev. Bailey would take
off his coat and tie
and go down to the basement
to shovel in more coal.
Only angels of the Lord
would do the above.
Only angels of the Lord
would be able to
get into the minds of common
folk and know what
would give them comfort.
But one day the Rev.
was called back.
I guess the Lord needed
him for a more
important mission.
Yes, his kidneys failed
and since there were no
dialysis machines at that time
he died.
Minnie was left at her post
to continue God's work
in our flock in Moline.
She did a great job
carrying on with out the Rev.

Angel Minnie continued to:
teach Sunday school
sing in the choir
raise money for our missionaries
play the piano or organ when called upon
and shout, "Amen! Amen! and
Hallelujah!" to add drama to
services.
Once, an unbeliever without any manners asked me,
"Buddy, you don't really believe in
angels and all the crap, do you?" I replied, "Yes
I do. In fact, I once washed dishes and
        hung out the clothes to dry with one."

The Lady who Lit the Menorah

In 1942 my grandmother
came to live with us.
Her full name was Elizabeth Ruth Mendell
and she was close to 75 years old.
She used to live in Chicago
until Grandpa Mendall died.
She was a very plump lady
with white hair and large black eyes.
She wore gold rimmed glasses
with bifocals.
She was a modest unassuming person
with an impish grin
and a willingness to listen.
She had been a book keeper
for her husband who
operated a drugstore and she had
a mind as sharp as a tack.
She didn't want to be a
burden and insisted on
helping pay our bills from money
left in my Grandpa's estate.
She spent most of her time
reading, sewing, guilting,
crocheting and gardening
in the summer.
The neighbors loved to chat with
her as she tended to the
roses dressed in an apron (to cover
her flower-printed dress),
long gloves and a wide straw sun
bonnet with a blue ribbon.

She seldom went to church
with us. She continued
to believe in and practice the
teachings of the Jewish
faith.
There was a synagogue in
Davenport but it was too
far away for her to go there
on a regular basis.
She took it upon herself the task
of educating her
grandchildren (me and Herby, my
brother) about the
Jewish holy days.
Oh Yahweh, I light the first candle.
I learned all about the following:
Pesach or Passover
Rosh HaShanah
Sukkoth
Hanukkah.
Oh Yahweh, I light the second candle.
She especially enjoyed
celebrating Hanukkah.
So when we put up our Christmas
tree, she always got out
her menorah.
Oh Yahweh. I light the third candle.
What? you say you do not know
what one looks like.

Well, it's a 8-branched candle stick,
with a place for a
"care candle" in the middle to
light up each candle.
Oh Yahweh, I light the forth candle.
The lighting of the candles
marks the
great victory of the Jews
over the forces
of Antiochus Epiphanes
in 168 B.C.
who wanted to destroy the
Jewish faith.
Oh Yahweh, I light the fifth candle.
I remember that the Christmas
of 1944 was an especially
emotional time for us because
the Battle of the Bulge
was going on during the holiday.
Oh Yahweh, I light the sixth candle.
Everyone was staying turned
to the radio to hear
the latest news about the battle.
And, they were praying that
the German advance would
be stopped.
Oh Yahweh, I light the seventh candle.

That year, as Grandma Mendell
lit the candles,
she spoke of the parallels between
the struggle against Hitler
and the struggle against the forces
of Antiochus Epiphanes
in 168 B.C.
Oh Yahweh, I light the 8th candle.
I learned a lot from my
Grandma Mendel.
Yes, a very wise lady
who came into my life
and left so much
wisdom and sunshine.

The Departing Words
from the Conductor

We are pulling into Union Station in Los Angeles. Make sure
you have all your carry-on baggage with you before you get off
the Express. Head left to the rear of the car to disembark.

So, how do you feel after your long journey into human
emotions? Exhausted. Well, you should. You have felt all the
emotions of the poor souls who live on this planet.

What do you make of it? What — you say that life is tough.
I agree. There are a lot of ups and downs in the life experience.
It takes courage to get through it.

In my opinion a lot of what happens is due to luck.
You are at the right or wrong place at the right or wrong time.

Life is very much like roulette or a card game. If you get a
good hand or if the ball lands in the right place on the revolving
wheel, it is Lady Luck.

Yes, in life good things happen — even to those who are morally
evil—and bad things happen to good people. It's luck or fate.

I was one of the lucky ones. I was saved by some nuns.
Yes, the Sisters of the Precious Blood saved a two year old
from being killed by the Nazis.

So, what can we do about this surreal world? Well, be happy for those who experience moments of joy and happiness. But, also reach out and help those in physical and emotional pain . Be a kind stranger.

And, if you can't find others to help you do what you feel must be done to save or help others, then do it alone.

You may fail — be killed even. But rest assured the martyrs in Heaven will embrace you and sing your praises.

You will be remembered as are all those who helped save Jews, like me, during the HOLOCAUST.

Well, take care as you disembark.

HAVE A GOOD DAY! GOOD LUCK!

About the Author

B.G. Webb was born in Germany and brought to this country after the Night of the Broken Glass in 1938. He grew up in Moline, Illinois and earned a B.A. from Augustana College and a M.A. in history from the University of Illinois.

He taught social studies for thirty-three years, mainly at Webster Groves High School in St. Louis County. He has published many books about the common folk. He combines old photos with art and what he calls "Folk Poetry" to address themes about the human condition.

He has dedicated many of his works to the kind lady — Dorothy Irene Webb-- who raised him in Moline, Illinois. She was one of the granddaughters of Rebecca Hirshman who was of the Jewish faith.

Members of the Hirshman family were part of an underground movement to save Jews during the 1930s and 1940s. They worked with others—Catholics and Protestants-- who were shocked by the killing of Jews during Hitler's policy of ethnic cleansing

B.G.'s web site is: www.bgwebb folk and poetry.com

Printed in the United States
By Bookmasters